W9-ARE-170

RUSSIA

by Theresa Jarosz Alberti

The Child's World

Published by The Child's World®
1980 Lookout Drive • Mankato, MN 56003-1705
800-599-READ • www.childsworld.com

Acknowledgments
The Child's World®: Mary Berendes, Publishing Director
Red Line Editorial: Editorial direction
The Design Lab: Design
Amnet: Production

Design elements: Asaf Eliason/Shutterstock Images;
Shutterstock Images; M. Shcherbyna/Shutterstock Images
Photographs ©: Natalia Kostitcina/Shutterstock Images,
cover (right), 30; Asaf Eliason/Shutterstock Images, cover
(left center), 1 (bottom left), 17 (left); Shutterstock Images,
cover (left bottom), 1 (bottom right), 27; M. Shcherbyna/
Shutterstock Images, cover (left top), 1 (top), 17 (right);
iStockphoto, 5, 6-7, 8, 9, 11, 12, 13, 15, 16, 17
(bottom), 19, 21, 22, 23, 24, 25; Semenova Jenny/
Shutterstock Images, 26; Serr Novik/iStockphoto, 28; Iakov
Filimonov/Shutterstock Images, 29

ISBN 9781634070553
LCCN 2014959732

Printed in the United States of America
Mankato, MN
July, 2015
PA02268

ABOUT THE AUTHOR
Theresa Jarosz Alberti
is a writer living in
Minneapolis, Minnesota.
She has published four
children's books and one
book of poetry. She
is especially fond of
reading children's books,
even as a grown up!

ONE WORLD • MANY COUNTRIES

TABLE OF CONTENTS

ARCTIC
OCEAN

RUSSIA

ATLANTIC
OCEAN

PACIFIC
OCEAN

PACIFIC
OCEAN

INDIAN
OCEAN

SCALE

0   1000 Miles

0   1000 KM

N
W   E
S

SOUTHERN
OCEAN

Russia is the world's largest country. It is roughly double the size of Canada, which is the world's second-largest country. Russia's land crosses nine time zones. It has Europe's tallest peak and longest river. Russia also has the world's deepest lake.

FUN FACT

ONE WORLD • MANY COUNTRIES

CHAPTER 1

WELCOME TO RUSSIA!

The night air is crisp and cold. Crowds gather in Red Square. They are celebrating Russia's most important holiday of the year. It is New Year's Eve! Everyone is excited to start this ten-day holiday. It is time to celebrate, feast, relax, and spend time with family and friends.

Fireworks explode over Red Square on New Year's Eve.

Shortly before midnight, citizens listen to a speech by Russia's president. He talks about the events of the past year and plans for the coming year. When he finishes, the clock strikes midnight. Bells chime and fireworks light up Red Square.

In homes across Russia, children are especially excited about the New Year. That is when the magical Father Frost visits homes with his granddaughter, the Snow Maiden. They bring gifts for the children. Families also decorate fir trees and prepare feasts.

Russia has been through challenging times. For almost 70 years it was one of many

countries in the Union of Soviet Socialist Republics (USSR). The USSR was ruled by the **Communist** Party. Under communism, citizens had few freedoms. The USSR broke apart into several countries in 1991. Today, Russia and the other countries have separate governments.

Life has changed for the citizens of Russia. There is much to celebrate every New Year's Eve.

A Russian girl receives her gifts from Father Frost and the Snow Maiden.

CHAPTER 2

THE LAND

The Caspian Sea is the world's largest inland body of water. It covers 1.4 million square miles (3.6 million sq km).

Russia stretches across Europe and Asia. It is the largest country in the world. Russia shares borders with 14 countries. These countries include Norway, Finland, Estonia, Latvia, Lithuania, Poland, Belarus, Ukraine, Georgia, Azerbaijan, Kazakhstan, China, Mongolia, and North Korea.

Russia is also bordered by several bodies of water. Northern Russia borders the Arctic Ocean. The North Pacific Ocean forms Russia's eastern border. The Black Sea and the Caspian Sea are in western Russia.

Russia has many mountains. The highest peak is Mount Elbrus. It is an inactive volcano in the Caucasus Mountains. The Ural Mountains run through west-central Russia. These mountains form a long boundary line between Europe and Asia.

Twenty-two glaciers rest on the peaks of Mount Elbrus.

Russia has 2 million lakes. Lake Baikal is the world's deepest lake. It is 1 mile (1.6 km) at its deepest point. Lake Baikal is also large. It holds one-fifth of the world's fresh water.

Russia's climate varies. In the tundra it is dry, cold, and windy. The tundra is located north of the Arctic Circle. It is too cold for trees to grow there. Moss, lichens, and low shrubs are the only plant life.

South of the tundra is the taiga. It is also known as the boreal forest. It is one of the largest types of forests on Earth. It is extremely cold during the long winters. The summers are short and mild.

An area called the steppe is south of the taiga. The steppe is a large, cold grassland. Many areas of the steppe are very dry. The average rainfall is often less than 8 inches (20 cm) per year.

Russia is a land rich in natural resources. Russia produces about 20 percent of the world's natural gas and oil. Their large reserves fuel Russia's energy needs. Russia also **exports** oil and natural gas to other countries.

The steppe has rich soil that is good for growing plants.

Russia's land is also rich in other resources. It has coal, timber, and tin. Russia also has many materials used in construction. They include sand, clay, limestone, granite, and marble.

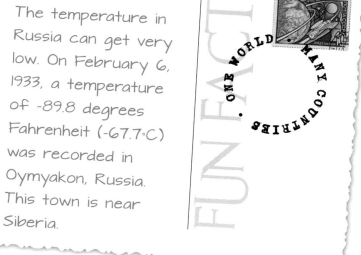

The temperature in Russia can get very low. On February 6, 1933, a temperature of -89.8 degrees Fahrenheit (-67.7°C) was recorded in Oymyakon, Russia. This town is near Siberia.

FUN FACT

ONE WORLD • MANY COUNTRIES •

CHAPTER 3

GOVERNMENT AND CITIES

More than 142 million people live in Russia. Moscow is its largest city. It is also the capital. Moscow has many famous **landmarks**. The most famous of these is Red Square. It is a large, open plaza. One of the buildings lining the square is the Kremlin. It is where Russia's government meets.

Another famous building in Red Square is St. Basil's Cathedral. Its colorful domes, towers, and arches rise above the square.

The Kremlin has served as a fortress and center of government since the 1300s.

St. Petersburg is the second-largest city in Russia. **Tsar** Peter the Great founded the city in 1703. Its most famous building is the Winter Palace. This was a home for Russian royalty. Many tourists now visit this large, beautiful palace.

Russia's government is a federation. In a federation, many districts join together to form a bigger country. These districts are broken down into republics, provinces, and territories.

Russian citizens elect the president. The president chooses a prime minister. The prime minister leads the government. Lawmakers and judges are also part of Russia's government.

Russia has not always been a federation. It used to be a communist republic. Russia's 70 years of communism still affect life in Russia today. Under communism, the government decided what people could read, watch, or listen to. The government owned the land, businesses, schools, and homes. Food was in short supply. Russians had little freedom.

St. Petersburg is located on the Neva River.

Pumps in western Siberia bring underground oil to the surface.

Communism ended in 1991. Today, Russians have more freedoms, food, and opportunity. The economy is growing. People can travel and practice their religion. It is not easy for Russians to forget their country's history. It is hard for Russians to trust the government. They find it hard to believe the freedoms will last.

Russia is a leading producer of oil and natural gas. It exports these fuels to other countries. Russia also exports coal, iron, steel, precious metals, wood, military equipment, and other resources. Countries such as China, Germany, the Ukraine, and Belarus buy these products.

Russia also **imports** goods from other countries. These goods include cars, medical supplies, vehicle parts, and computers. Most of Russia's imports come from the Netherlands, China, Germany, and the Ukraine.

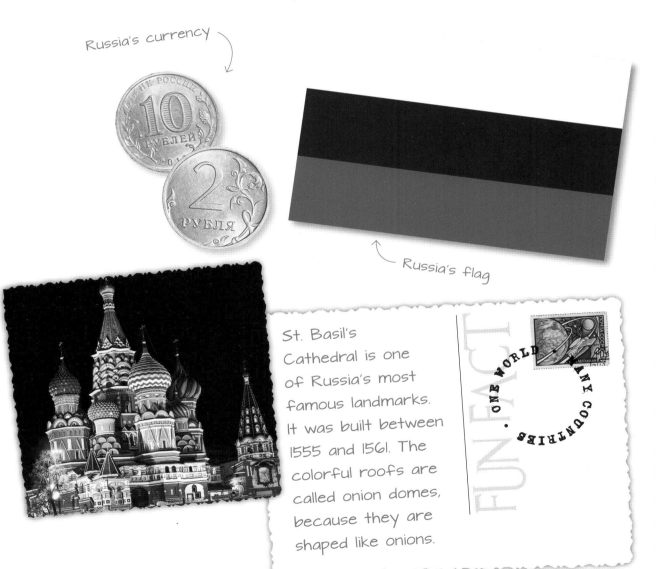

Russia's currency

Russia's flag

St. Basil's Cathedral is one of Russia's most famous landmarks. It was built between 1555 and 1561. The colorful roofs are called onion domes, because they are shaped like onions.

FUN FACT

ONE WORLD • MANY COUNTRIES

GLOBAL CONNECTIONS

Russia is a world leader. It has strength because of its size, resources, and powerful government. It has many connections with other countries.

Russia has developed **alliances** with many countries. India, China, Belarus, Iran, and Syria are Russian allies.

Alliances often change and shift over time. Russia and the United States have been allies at times. Other times there have been struggles between the two countries. Sometimes it is hard for two powerful countries to agree.

Russia also connects to the world through its **immigration** policy. It is second only to the United States in the number of immigrants entering the country. Many people from former countries in the USSR come to Russia. They can earn higher wages and have better living conditions in Russia.

CHAPTER 4

PEOPLE AND CULTURES

In Russia, 77 percent of the people are Russian. People of other nationalities live in Russia, too. There are Ukrainians, Tartars, Bashkirs, Chuvash, Chechens, and more.

Despite the cold weather, many Russians enjoy being outdoors.

Russian is the official language of Russia. Russian uses the Cyrillic alphabet. Some Cyrillic letters are the same as English letters. Other letters look different. For example, Д sounds like a *d* and П sounds like a *p*.

People in other countries often study Russian. Some are drawn to it because of Russia's important position in the world. Others want to read famous works of Russian literature. One famous Russian author is Leo Tolstoy. He wrote the books *War and Peace* and *Anna Karenina*. Many people think they are two of the world's best novels.

The majority of Russians follow the Russian Orthodox Church. This religion follows the beliefs and customs of the early Christian church. Under communism, religion was discouraged. Some people were punished for practicing their religion. Many Russians gave up their religion or kept their beliefs a secret.

Today, people no longer have to practice their religion in secret. Citizens are free to go to church. The number of people practicing the Russian Orthodox religion is growing. Russia also has Muslims and other types of Christians.

Russians celebrate several holidays throughout the year. New Year's Day is a favorite holiday. February 23 is Defender of

Worshippers pray at Kazan Cathedral in St. Petersburg, Russia.

the Motherland Day. Men and boys are honored with gifts and cards for their military service. Sometimes there are parades. Most men serve in Russia's military.

In March, Russians celebrate International Women's Day. On this holiday, all females are honored. Mothers, daughters, grandmothers, sisters, and girlfriends are celebrated. Families often share a meal and visit friends. Women receive flowers, chocolate, cards, poetry, or a day of rest.

A girl carries a plate of pancakes in honor of Maslyanitsa. This holiday marks the end of winter.

Maslyanitsa is Russia's oldest folk holiday. It is held the week before **Lent**. Pancakes are served with honey, **caviar**, fresh cream, and butter. People celebrate, dance, sing, and wear traditional Russian clothing.

Russia Day is one of Russia's newest holidays. It is celebrated on June 12. This day honors Russia's independence.

It is a day citizens show their love for Russia. Sometimes there are track and field events. People make special foods and set off fireworks. Russians are proud of their country's achievements and creativity.

A traditional folk craft in Russia is making nesting dolls. They are called matryoshka. The dolls are carved from wood and then painted by hand.

FUN FACT

ONE WORLD · MANY COUNTRIES

CHAPTER 5

DAILY LIFE

Dachas are similar to cabins. They are small homes used for vacations.

In Russian cities, most people live in apartments. In the countryside, Russians might live in a house or cottage. Some families in the city also have a small country home with a garden. This is called a *dacha*. *Dachas* are used for vacations or as summer homes.

From an early age, Russian children learn the importance of wearing warm clothing in Russia's frigid winters.

Most Russians wear clothing similar to what is worn in the United States. Clothing must be warm because of the cold climate. Russians often wear clothing made of wool or fur. An *ushanka* is a fur-lined hat with ear flaps. It helps keep out the brutal cold.

A woman wearing a kokoshnik

Russians also wear traditional clothing. It is often worn as part of a performance or cultural event. Women and girls wear colorful dresses with embroidery and decorations. Sometimes they wear a special headdress called a *kokoshnik*. It is tall and ribbons tie at the back of the head into a big bow.

Men and boys wear a bright shirt called a *kosovorotka*. They wear this along with a belt, pants, and boots.

The long winters and short growing seasons affect what Russians eat. Foods that grow well in Russia are potatoes, cabbage, carrots, beets, and apples. Fresh fruits and vegetables can be hard to find in the winter.

One of Russia's best-known ballets is the Nutcracker. Pyotr Ilyich Tchaikovsky composed the music for the ballet in 1892. Today, this ballet is a classic throughout the world.

Some of Russia's foods have become well known around the world. *Borsht* is a soup made with beets, beef broth, and other vegetables. Russia is famous for its caviar. Caviar is tiny fish eggs from sturgeon, salmon, and other fish. Caviar is an expensive treat.

The arts are an important part of Russia's culture. Russia is known for its excellence in ballet. Classical music, opera, theater, and literature entertain Russians through the long winters. Russians also enjoy watching international chess tournaments.

Skiing is a popular pastime in Russia. This boy is skiing down a mountain near Sochi, Russia.

Because of Russia's cold climate, winter sports are popular. Hockey, cross-country skiing, and figure skating are popular. Other popular sports in Russia are weightlifting, tennis, basketball, volleyball, boxing, and football. Russian football is the same as American soccer.

In its history, Russia has gone through many changes. Today the nation is growing. Its people have more freedoms than ever before.

DAILY LIFE FOR CHILDREN

Russian children attend school from ages six to 17. They study literature, the Russian language, history, math, and science.

With Russia's long winters, playing in the snow is a favorite activity of Russian children. They make snowmen and throw snowballs. Some cities even build statues, small castles, or slides out of snow. Children go sledding and cross-country skiing. They play boot hockey by sliding around on hard-packed snow. Families enjoy bonfires outside.

Older women often wear a large scarf on their head that is tied under their chin. The head covering is called a *babushka*. It is the Russian word for "grandmother."

FUN FACT

ONE WORLD · MANY COUNTRIES

FAST FACTS

Population: 142 million

Area: 6.6 million square miles (17 million sq km)

Capital: Moscow

Largest Cities: Moscow and St. Petersburg

Form of Government: Federation

Language: Russian

Trading Partners: China, the Netherlands, and Germany

Major Holidays: New Year's Eve, Defender of the Motherland Day, and International Women's Day

National Dish: Borscht (a rich soup made from beets, beef broth, and vegetables)

A Russian girl in traditional folk clothing

GLOSSARY

alliances (uh-LIE-uhns-ez) Alliances are agreements between two or more nations to work together in peace. Russia has many alliances.

caviar (kah-VEE-ar) Caviar are cured fish eggs eaten as a delicacy. Russia is famous for its caviar.

communist (KAHM-yoo-nist) A communist government owns all the land, houses, and factories. It shares the country's profits equally among the citizens. Russia was a communist country for many years.

exports (ek-SPORTS) When a country exports goods, it sells them to other countries. Russia exports many products.

immigration (IM-ih-gray-shun) Immigration is when people move from one county to another to live. Russia's immigration policy allows people to enter the country.

imports (ihm-PORTS) When a country imports goods, it buys them from other countries. Russia imports many goods.

landmarks (LAND-marks) Landmarks are buildings or other places of historical or cultural importance. St. Basil's Cathedral and the Kremlin are landmarks in Moscow.

Lent (lent) Lent is a time of fasting and prayer to prepare for Easter. Lent lasts 40 days.

tsar (tsahr) A tsar is the name for the emperor of Russia. Russia no longer has a tsar as its leader.

TO LEARN MORE

BOOKS

Adams, Simon. *Changing World: Russia.*
Mankato, MN: Arcturus Publishing. 2010.

Marshall, Deb. *Russia.* New York: AV2 by Weigl, 2013.

Russell, Henry. *Countries of the Word: Russia.*
Washington D.C.: National Geographic Society, 2008.

WEB SITES

Visit our Web site for links about Russia: **childsworld.com/links**

Note to Parents, Teachers, and Librarians: We routinely verify our Web links to make sure they are safe and active sites. So encourage your readers to check them out!

INDEX

28.65